A SMALL ESSAY ON THE
LARGENESS
OF LIGHT
AND OTHER POEMS

A SMALL ESSAY ON THE
LARGENESS
OF LIGHT

AND OTHER POEMS

Daniel David Moses

Library and Archives Canada Cataloguing in Publication

Moses, Daniel David, 1952-
    A small essay on the largeness of light and other poems / Daniel David
Moses.

Poems.
ISBN 978-1-55096-301-4

    I. Title.

PS8576.O747S63 2012   C811'.54   C2012-906211-1

Design and Composition by Hourglass Angels~mc
Typeset in Fairfield and Mariposa fonts at the Moons of Jupiter Studios
Cover Photograph by Vladimir Piskunov. Printed by Imprimerie Gauvin

Published by Exile Editions Ltd ~ www.ExileEditions.com
144483 Southgate Road 14 – GD, Holstein ON, N0G 2A0
Printed and Bound in Canada; Publication Copyright © Exile Editions, 2012

The publisher would like to acknowledge the financial support of the Canada
Council for the Arts, the Government of Canada through the Canada Book
Fund (CBF), the Ontario Arts Council, and the Ontario Media Development
Corporation, for our publishing activities.

Canadian Sales: The Canadian Manda Group, 165 Dufferin Street,
Toronto ON M6K 3H6   www.mandagroup.com   416 516 0911

North American and International Distribution, and U.S. Sales:
Independent Publishers Group, 814 North Franklin Street,
Chicago IL 60610   www.ipgbook.com   toll free: 1 800 888 4741

for My Sister

I

II

III

IV

Daniel David Moses recites three poems:
scan this QR, or access the video via URL at
www.tinyurl.com/ThreePoems

I

RISING SONG

Yes, your body hates the way the night damp,
Leaking in through the thin slit of window

This early, even this late in spring, breaks
The proverbial log of good sleep up

Briskly into shivering—but your head
Knows simply shutting the window down tight

Would be warmer and you might even get
Back to that dream. Vertical in your bed,

Uncovered and chilly, with blood tingling
Into, finding your feet, Sleepy Head, meet

Across the sill something that will wake
Your love up instead, mist golden as a gong

That the light, still horizontal, brushes
By like a breeze, making it ring—bird song!

ONE SOVIET-ERA WINTER

For a moment or three, the sun
         Stretched out in front of the fridge, then
Skedaddled back into the blue
         February sky. Clouds on high,
Cotton batting for sure, were up

         For playing hide-and-seek. Which left
You lazing on the linoleum,
         Warm as cat's fur, apprehending,
Therefore, your eyes closed, how
         That fridge-motor hummed as if it were

A purr. Where, you wondered—you rolled
         Over and sat up, following
The thought—has that old Sputnik,
         Your all-black (but for a frosted
Star at her throat) house cat got to?

         In that season for staying in,
The cracked window opened onto
         A drift of snow across the back
Yard, its tail flicking, icy
         Irritation, then and again.

SONG OF A SCENT

Tonight the boy from the country
Resists this list the Ex gives off.
His nose knows the month isn't just

Cotton candy or lavendered
Ladies or morning coffee. None
Of that is enough when the cup

His head is once held dust and straw
And his Granddad's yellow roses.
No, even fireworks blooming

Overhead, gunpowder stinking,
Can't prove themselves sufficient to
His nose's way of drinking. Then

A gust that is all of August
Fills up his head, the late blooming
Flower Lake Ontario is.

A FRISSON IN GRANGE PARK

The man out for a walk takes that path through Grange Park
      Under the chestnut trees so thick with foliage
They swallow up the thin electric streetlight shine,

Leaving the man stepping through a dark, though cool and
      Still, all about breathing, yes, that also seems, thanks
To the flowers, pale as mist and motionless

On limbs that rise above his head, to be keeping
      Watch. He turns from the one star he's spotted on high
Towards the mumbling traffic over on Beverley,

Entertaining the thought of birds of prey, owls most
      Likely, perched in the dark—Though they don't usually
Gather in flocks, do they?—taking his movements in

With their untwinkling eyes. Then out on the sidewalk,
      He stops to catch his breath, to button his coat, right
To the collar, covering up his naked throat.

TWINKLE

By day, stars
        May be seen,
Reflections
        Deep in wells.
Is that true?

So they say.
        Take a look.
The dark at
        The nadir
Trembles with

A single
        Pale petal.
Is that you?
        —Your face blind
With questions.

BLUES AROUND A REARVIEW MIRROR

Autumn's overripe
Sun dropped long ago. What
A splash it made, what
A mess. The moon,

Too new to float
That long through
The congealing, blackening
Wreck of November sky,

Bright mote in the rearview's eye,
Now says adieu too.
We two, stuck
Behind the steering wheel

With no time for goodbyes,
Pass on, pass
By, facing the flowing high
Way night, the head-

And taillights
Of other survivors.
Meanwhile our sighs
Are silvering the glass,

Fogging the windshield,
Too, into a mirror
Where our destination
Appears, a ghost

Among stars. The map's
Here on my lap. Where
Are these abandoned
Barns, this land of dead

Elms? How will we cross
All this drift
Wood at sea in shadows?
Then pumpkins the colour

Of flame, a peripheral
Vision, buoy
Up from the deep
Blue field to the right.

Hold tight, they seem to say,
The bright bud of
The sun will rise anew.
You believe them.

IN THE DON VALLEY

How hard it rained last night!
November out to
Extinguish all light. What dark

Habitations trees now
Are in the dawn, last colours
Shards in the iced-over

Puddles at my feet
As I run—except for this one
Glowing apple

Still holding on despite
The season, whole and bright
As our breath in the sun.

POOL BLUES

How many lengths of blue
      Chlorinated water
Have you done? It's laid you

Out in the naked sun.
      Listen to the plash as
Other swimmers push end

To end. The sky is blue
      Enough today to dye
Any cloth—that red kite,

Say, playing the hot wind,
      Flickers its tail, such
A lonely and purple

Spermatozoa. How
      Quick a wisp of batting
Cloud is gone in the light.

How long before we too
      Evaporate? Or will
We never get that bright?

BLUES IN AUGUST

The sky, my shirt, a chicory flower—
The colour of lowering hopes. None from

Now on will fly that high or be this warm
Or manage such a bloom. Look. Already

The lake's more delicate hues choose to ride
—Suicides!—waves into the breakwater.

Boo hoo. What else can you expect? Falling,
And darkness. A stiffening in your neck.

THE PLOUGHMAN AT MIDDLE AGE

I lost myself this morning,
Slipping the yoke my body
Was and scooting up into
      The cumulostratus sphere

Above the lake. The fields
There opened up like mother-
Of-pearl—so I laid down
      My ache. And when a ray of light

Poked through, tagged my shoulder and
Then withdrew, I found myself
A kid again, 'it' in a game
      Of hide-and-seek. So where would

The sun go to ground? I found
And followed the new furrow
A flush of bright water had
      Cut right through the afternoon.

And I was off, running again,
Yes, racing the sun for
Home, the pair of us laughing
      The whole way back to the barn.

WHY THE COW MOOS

The lost calf, found,
      Electric green
Flies a tarnished
      Hum in its mouth,
Winged pennies

On its eyes, pays
      You back fuck all
For the hours
      That you spent criss-
Crossing the swamp,

Boots sinking step
      After step, sucked
Down by the muck.
      Some part of you
Is still sinking

As this small change
      Gang rises up
In unwelcome
      Greeting. Your gut
Might just return

The favour. How
     Strange, this humming's
Become a calf's
     Last laugh, a stink
Of soured milk.

BUZZ

It's not just me, there's also you,
Both of us up and unable
To take a break, you from buzzing

That ten-watt bulb, me from being
Awake. Why do I think the two
Situations are linked? What do

I care? The thought that a fly might
Be stuck in some facsimile
Of a tragic plot, *Electron*

and Nucleus, the twain never
To meet, ought not to bore me. Love,
Even one so meagre, deserves,

I was taught, a consummation.
But what your motive toward the light
Gets from me is irritation.

If you tick against that glass once
More, I'm afraid it might push me
Through one of the many new cracks

In my old composure. Oh, tick

Again and the live wiring of
My brain will short out, electrons

Doing their bit for comedy,
A sputtered climax, which would, yes,
Improve on this dead end we're in.

I lay me down, praying you will
Tick once more, even while the buzz
Of reason reminds me none of

My prayers have been answered before.
To calm me more it questions why
I don't try that switch by the door.

I don't know any more. I don't
Know. Even with my body so
Far away, it should be easy

As breaking glass. A forefinger
And thumb made out of the darkness
Pinching us out of existence—

THE LONGEST NIGHT

I have grown too
Familiar

With the end of
The year. I no

Longer need to
Pretend I'm friends

With the darkness
Here. No, ours is

As perfect
A civility

As you might
Expect—excepting

The chilly
Condescension of

Stars. All I have
Yet to forget.

II

MY PARENTS VERSUS LYNX RUFUS

Was the night ripping apart?
        The conversation died as
Dad tried to explain that pain

        Tearing through the blue evening
As just the cry of a now
        Very rare cat. But then Mom,

Following the spot his flash
        Light sent searching through the dark
Of the fallow field back

        Of the house, shook her head and
Whispered *It's awful*. And for
        The long, still moment that pair

Of eyes were open out there,
        Looking back and reflecting
The light, needle bright, leaving

        Night darker, I couldn't find
The thread of conversation,
        Even in the clarity

The yard light provided. Mom
       Must have been the one to get
The small talk started. The news

       Of common, family things,
I'm sure, sewed up whole the cloth
       Of that summer night again.

TWO VIEWS OF THE ECLIPSE

for E.C.L.

We dream in black and white, or so the experts say.
　　　　We also seem to live our days a lot that way.
But tonight, this black and white held-breath of a scene,

A Milky Way haze laid down over the farm but
　　　　High overhead—this can't be our dream since we're not
Yet asleep, not yet abed. Since the phasing face

Of the Moon makes her seem both awake and asleep
　　　　All at once, though she's full and travelling the sky,
The epitome of tranquility even

Orbiting through the zenith, she gets the credit
　　　　Or blame for this dream. But why are we boys in it?
After all the blacks and whites of *The Late Late Show,*

We've had our night's fill of fiction, so we're up and
　　　　Itching for a truth not found on televisions
And expecting it to happen in this moonlit

View where a total eclipse's been predicted.
　　　　The girls—your wife and my sister—hours ago
Headed off to bed, weren't very interested

In some black and white and rare in a lifetime trick
        The Moon might pull when their own colourful dreams
Were just pillows away. When experts do allow

That colour can show up in dreams, at their junctures
        Or their ends, maybe it's because women like these
Keep dreaming—like the Moon—outside their expertise.

Where is she now? My binoculars locate her
        Between earthshine and umbra, but there's a colour
Blurring her face—I can't get it in focus. You

Give it a try and with a laugh start telling me
        About craters and seas, sharp and up close, clear as
—I almost see—a photograph. The one problem

—It's not new—is how the scene continues for you
        Black and white, clarity being a benefit
Tonight, we're reminded, of being colour-blind.

Neither of us can see after all what the whole
        Truth might be. Could it help you to know that I think
The Moon's burnt orange colour almost matches your wife's

Hair? Do you detect the dream's end or juncture now?
        Tomorrow morning, in the full colours of high
Summer, awake again (the old Moon far below

The horizon), over bowls of cold cereal,
We'll share our observations. Do you think
Together we'll be able to tell the truth then?

CAROL OF THE RAIN

Yes, the old woman's ready,
A lady in her chair. All
That's necessary now to
      Get her there is a shawl made

Of lace laid around her thin
Shoulders—just that and a push.
For though it's the holiday
      And December, her only

Complaint could be wet, not cold,
Drizzle so light, she might not
Even get splashed. He hurries.
      The wheels of her chair hiss

Across asphalt and the rain
Flies up, the first to greet her.
In the banquet hall, festive
      With little star lights, the boy

Parks her at the head table
Where someone's gotten her tea
And raised voices compliment
      Her shawl and give all their best

Wishes. The boy's the only
One who saw how the rain kissed
Her cheek and made her smile
　　　Like a meek, joy-filled child.

LOVE ISN'T A TRUCK

She makes a fist and the fist
Punches the steering wheel
As if Dad's old pickup truck
Were acting up and needed
To be brought somehow to heel.

What luck we're in park outside
Granma's shop. If we'd been on
The road, we might have ended
Up upended in a ditch.
The wheel's vibration stops.

—*Where did that come from?*—The fist
Unclenches and waves as if
Nothing's wrong. There's no need to
Worry. So I'll wait a while
For the gist of the story.

It's not exactly Dad's truck
She hit. It's more her own heart
And the confused directions
It's repeating she's trying
To get at. It has to change

Its beating or she'll never
Be able to think clearly
Enough to find her way back.
She's on the path unbeaten.
Organize a search party.

The Dodge just has to do since
She can't beat up on the source
Of her bewilderment, he
Who told lies. Or on the fool
Animal who believed him,

Her heart. The guy took his own
Back, leaving hers alone, closed
On air, dryness, promises,
Then opening like a hand
Or eyes, a mouth, for a bone.

Even after it found out
About the wife, after he
Began beating his retreat,
Her heart wanted to follow,
Broke out tongues to say so

And still continues to beg.
She just wants to shut it up.
Is the strategy working?
She's not any less lost. Is
Bruising her own bones enough

Of a distraction? Broken
Parts of her are whispering,
Arguing, gossiping, off
In the bush, insect noise
Often too sharp to ignore.

She has to spend so much time
Pretending not to hear what
She hears, though the voices have
Half convinced her it might be
Good, since no remnants of road,

Sand or corduroy, present
Her with a way out of her
Dilemma, to just lie down
And sink under the covers
The swampland offers. But Dad's

Old truck is evidence she
Once and could again travel
A world without what's his name.
—*So where're we goin'?*—She starts
The truck up, shifts into gear,

Pulling up to the end of
The drive. She checks to her left,
I glance to my right.—*Any*
Thing comin'?—*Clear*, I reply
And we're out on the gravel,

Travelling a road as straight
As it's narrow, home, across
The reserve in our Dad's truck,
Me never doubting our luck,
Sure we'll both arrive alive.

THE ORCHARD SONG

The farmer's son
    Climbs up among
The branches of the night.
    He's always dreamed
Of harvesting
    A moon so sweet, so ripe.

    His eyes are full of silver
        —He's always had far sight.
    Beyond his father's land
        He sees
    A city made of light.

How many moons
    Will be enough
For him to leave the farm?
    All the taxes
The land carries,
    The old man's broken bones.

    The old man's eyes are water,
        That second kind of sight.
    Beneath the tree of night
        He met
    A woman made of clay.

The farmer's wife
    Will lose her son
—He'll tarnish in the town.
    He'll spend himself,
He'll lose his way,
    Counterfeiting the moon.

The woman's eyes are oceans
    —She's always seen her boy
Climb up the tree of day,
    At play
—The apple of her eye.

ONCE UPON AN EVENING OUT ALONG SIXTH LINE

I'm out for my run, at dusk instead of at dawn,
        Along the gravel road I used to bike to school
And chance upon the old man, my father, also
        Out at that hour, taking his constitutional.

        Already he's so far ahead, silhouetted
Against the sunset, and apparently in such
        A mad hurry—strange in a guy over eighty—
I fear I won't ever be able to catch up.

So I imagine Dad wanting to say hello,
        Stopping and turning back, though I know the night can't
That easily be put on pause, though it's catching
        Up with both of us, though my Dad—like that, he's gone.

        My hope is to hurry to where I saw him last,
To maybe stand again on the road's shoulder and
        Catch the rough edge of his voice untangling itself,
Calling my name from these dark woods across the ditch.

Nothing stirs, not even a hint of Vitalis
        Lingering to liven up the air. I keep on
Up the road, wonder where he's got to, still certain
        He has to be somewhere. That path, overgrown now,

That led to the sandpit? Or out in the clearing
The pit was before that, where on summer mornings
        It used to be good mushroom picking, where by night
With luck you'd espy the brief pulse of fireflies.

From that fallow field with the sun down I know
        He'd see the Big Dipper, be able to follow
Its famous vector all the way to Polaris,
        And maybe remember the radio silent

        Flight his PBY Catalina took the night
Nothing happened, his gunner sights on such stars
        And the tarmac in Iceland. He never said word
One about any of those missions, and had no

Comment on my handbook of the constellations.
        The boy who riffled through its pictures, who saw on
Past the Big Dipper to the bear, Ursa Major,
        Now lifts up his eyes to a decondensing trail.

        He finishes my run, stumbling home in the dark,
No longer sure that the road's up ahead. Stars can't
        Really be trusted, not like suns, so from now on
He plans to take his constitutional at dawn.

SOME EGGS BEFORE BREAKFAST

A sudden killdeer cries
And flickers by, trying
To get and keep my eyes
On her and off her (must
Be) nearby nest. Which would
Be better accomplished

If her further sleight of
Wing—dragging one along
As if it's broken—had
Not been written up so
Often and if I weren't
More drawn, jogging along

The gravel shoulder in
The dawn, to what the sun's
Putting on display. Night
Has left me so empty,
Not even Birdy's clutch
Of (likely) four eggs would

Be filling enough to
Redirect my gaping
When this sunrise seems—as
It does today astride
The steaminess of the mist
The field of corn e-

Mits—to be a yolk of
Celestial proportions.
Don't waste your tricks on me,
Dear Bird. Such subtleties
Are mere shade in the light
Of this clearly bigger

Than my stomach thing. Not
Even my own dear Mom's
Worn caveat can hold
Beside this impression
The ripening corn's doing,
Lifting its dried-out, own

Broken-wing leaves into
The day's first yellow rays
And breeze so wildly. Out
Of night's frying pan dreams
Into day's wider-eyed
Fiery imaginings,

Am I the one cracking,
A good egg ready to
Be fried by his own fast-
Induced fantasies? But
This breeze, running across
The corn, extinguishing

Those images, yields
This soft, gently mocking
Laughter and a more hard-
Boiled me. I slacken
My stride. Wherever you
Hide in the line of tricks,

In this unwieldly, half
Visible world, Dear Bird,
I owe you for putting
Me on the alert. What
I'm hearing now, this full
Silence, draws a smiley

Face on my shell. This last
Mile back to the house
My ears are uncluttered.
So I'll hear my own old
Mother, nested in her
Soft and regular snores

When I arrive. What will
I tell her when—"I'm still
alive!"—she wakes, ready
For my coffee? Sometimes
It takes imagined eggs
To make a real breakfast.

SONG OFF YOUR FEET

I thought you walked
On wings, fine-boned,
Strong, sure things. Pale
As roots, perhaps
From wintering
In rubber boots.

How glad I am
The sun had come back
North, so glad
Those feet are bare
And touch the earth.
And then you speak,

A joke, a line,
Almost a poem, what
With the words
Dancing in feet out
Of your mouth,
Sprouting green,

A vine up my spine,
Your words strong and
Fine and sure as
A sunflower. Who
Needs wings now?
In my boney

Head, I know
If I can just walk
Beside you, I'll
Never again feel
Any need
To leave the ground.

LAMENT UNDER THE MOON

On the lookout beside
     The wide river of night,
Seeing how the moon's

Reflection swims, I'd rather
     Be certain about where
In midcurrent, in mid-

Crossing you are. So far
     Ahead—though you're younger—
Into and through the waning

Light. Too soon you'll dive
     Underwater, try with
One breath to reach the far

Shore and not leave the moon
     Crazy in your wake. You
Can't wait for me. Too late,

Too late. Too soon you'll rest
     Beyond the moon, another
Great Bear made of stars.

III

A BARN OFF THE 401

Hurry past the weathered
       Boards—for there are no words
In whitewash now, no names

Or questions stretched across
       The ingrained red. The man
Who wanted an answer,

Who painted *Where will you*
       be in eternity?
Is gone already, just like

His farm. Only the wind
       Remains, wandering
In the fallow fields

Beyond, too despondent
       To do more than sigh. Why
Is it we never know

Who they were, farmers and
       Their sons? Wind, settle down,
Be a wreath for this barn.

STARLING STREET

Under the blizzard's
Beating
Wings, the rush hour

Slows and
Staggers, coughs and
Complains. What good is it,

Headlights
Blinking on,
With nothing to see? The night

Coming to ground
With talons
Comes down blindingly.

And you pushing
Home on foot through
This world made of

Slush, windshield-
Wiperless, what else
Can you do

But lose the way? How
Uncool
Hypothermia

Will be. Mush, mush. Turn
Aside. Down this street,
A dark

Untenanted
Department store
Provides a lee. Snow

Comes down like bright down
Around you
Under the one

Streetlight here. Cries
Are descending too
From that flock

Contending along
The sills. In your palm,
The flakes

Unmake, melt down,
And in your ears,
Argument sings:

Rest your wings, oh
Daughters, oh sons
Of the waters!

OUR LINDA'S DREAM

The city drowns in rain
But this time it's a dream.
      Never wide awake would
She have ever dared wear
Moccasins on the street.

Even now her dream self
Hesitates, day dreams feet
      Laced into running shoes,
White and new, about to
Step out into the wet.

But the foot that contacts
The concrete sports hide and
      No threat of soak or slide
Or sideways glance any
Longer impedes her stride.

In her dream moccasins
She walks on the water
      As the city subsides.
She'll even dare wear them
On the wide-awake street.

A SHINE HUNG OVER MONTREAL

A haze of fluff—as if the air's
Not already pale enough!
Even on the *Ile Sainte Hélène*,

There's no escape from the reek and
Ruckus the city throws up. Talk
About morning breath—but all day—

Talk about intoxication,
The unsteady way the city
Stumbles along the horizon.

If only one could lie still, pool
In the shade downhill in the lee
Of rocks away from the sun's u.

V., forgetting the breeze that picks
Cotton off the break of poplars,
Tossing it up over the white

Heads of clover like angelic
Aspirin—one might sing along.
But it flies down your throat, a dry

Little bird you can't swallow and
Even that pool whose cool one thought
One might mirror disappears, its face

—Like the one from last night?—about
Lost in the soft irritation.
Hair of the bitch. That brewery

Across the *Courant Sainte Marie*,
Sign edited down by the trunk
Of a tree to just the word *Mo on*,

Doesn't please or amuse—scratches
The mind's eye, a shard in the haze,
Empty as this glass afternoon.

THE ENDS OF A PICNIC

Oh you're black and lucky, bird, strutting through the grass
Out into the sun—and away from an impasse
In conversation, from words gone blue, too sour
In the heat, ever to chew on, let alone eat.

We could be lucky too or bright with a slew of
Picnic fixings to squeeze, in lieu, into our beaks.
How nice to have pre-sliced cheese and cold cuts to share,
I've always said. How nice to break bread. You don't need

Knives to—and chance is with us, since we did forget
To bring a blade along into the shade today
Where the blades of grass won't be cutting off any
Arteries. Wit's evident too in these far too

Few sweet grapes included on the menu. Or is
That irony one only I have the taste for?
We're sharing the relative calm of a blanket
Spread out in the public sun but the appetites,

Yes, the vocabulary, we held in common
Are gone or in need of translation. Is that why
You're here, you dark and winged thing, to bring some sense
Back into our sentences, our heads? To feed off

All the clever words we said? To take them up through
The haze of poplar fluff and leave the silences
We're waiting in white as the face of the pond is
Under a cover of the stuff? No reflections

Show up there or here unless the wind or we stir—
And who dares at these temperatures? Only you
And that one young man who also strutted over
The grass, just as cocky as that red and yellow off

Your wings. He made the trek all the way uphill out
Of the shade and now, bending over the spouting
Fountain there, like the sun thirsty on his brown skin
For bright salt, he begins sucking up that jet as

If it really were a spring, really were that sort
Of first ever clear flowing, like the one that once
Upon a time got the two of us going, yes,
Unafraid to go along on this escapade.

HOW TO MAKE A FISH SWEAT

Jigging through the haze overhead, the metal of
Stars, so far away, won't lure more than eyes from bed.
      The rest of our bodies, spread out at the bottom

Of the night, even up on the seventeenth floor,
Dive after the ice in the depths of tall, empty
      Glasses, searching for an alcohol clear shiver.

We find instead a stir in the heavy water
We're made of, a hot flow of salt rising into
      Muscles, nostrils, the cheeks of our shining faces.

The current the fan on the sill propels never
Will dry the one inside our skins. Oh our tongues shine
      Silver with the taste, spooning the submarine night.

AN OLDER HARVEST KIND OF MOON

Smell those fried onions. You know no
      Other aroma can rise to
Such heights above the fairground slew,

Even though you might prefer, oh,
      Lavender, popcorn, even horse
Manure, yes, after this half hour

Hanging at the Ferris wheel's
      Top, too high up to hear just why
The ride's shuddered and died—my guess

Is we're out of gas—when hunger,
      Sensing onions, only wonders,
Mouth watering, Can hamburger

Be far below? And we know Yes
      Is the answer. Only a tease
Gets up to these nostrils. Forget

About your gut. Forget about
      What the moon does too, buttery
Bright and rising to just our height

Off the horizon, offering
        Celestial rings of onion.
Forget about eating the moon.

Oh if only our feet were on
        The ground. Then we could be milling
Around too—the living giving

Thanks for having more than moonlight
        On our plates. But that's not our fate
Tonight. Tonight in silhouette

We're the dark meat on the moon plate
        And scavengers await our fall.
See. They're the ones with the recessed

Incisors. Sit still. Don't rock. Let
        The moon inspire their songs. Oh what
Repairs can be taking this long?

MOON OF THE WINDFALLEN

The moon, so ripe on its stem,
He wants to be a kid and
Clamber through the branches of

The tree of night again, needs
To look out through the topmost limbs
At the illuminated

Farm, a harvest of many
Moons, as the saying goes, safe
In a six-quart basket hung

From his arm. How long did
He think that harvest would last?
How much did it profit him

Once he'd been taxed off the land,
Once he'd landed with his boots
Here on the pavement? How long,

He's wondering, has it been
That I've been here? So long
He can no longer see the lights

Of the city, flickering
To fullness after sunset,
As anything other than

Counterfeit. The real moon's
Light, in his experience,
Never tarnished anything.

These shadows thrown around him
Are branches no boy ever
Will climb. The old moon, this time

Round, rises to the zenith.
The man enters the corner
Store, hungry for pale apples.

MY DISCOVERY OF AMERICA

The bluster of speeches blew over my head
Those February weeks we crouched, posted
To the edge of the legislature floor.

What were we hearing, there and then, young men
Of twelve or thirteen, when we weren't on runs,
Carrying message slips up to the hacks

Who crewed the backbenches? The words that steered
The province's ship yielded nothing
I've used projecting the map of my life.

Our own expedition over the noon
Hour, equipped with brown bag lunches and books,
Put us ashore in the nearly silent,

Almost uninhabited museum's
Interior, where we whispered. What you
Wanted me to see was a marble bust.

The throat of Aurelius, I recall,
And your untanned wrist showed the same thin veins.
And we also found—was it underground?—

An old diorama where mannequin
Indians offered up white and bruised beads,
Replicas of wampum. Though those relics

Indicated the direction, inland,
Up the river of bruises and veins, we
Didn't understand. Then duty called us

Back aboard and our season as pages
Ended. So that land got left unexplored
Until one year I needed to get lost,

To find myself in that territory,
Carrying those relics like a compass.
I also found myself then recalling

And calling out the name of the boy who'd
Gone overboard with me. Had we known how
To swim then, we might have discovered

Those unsettled headwaters together.
Part of me still is whispering, laying
Claim to that green place in his memory.

AYISHA IN THE DARKROOM

Rumours of the death of painting
Were alive and well established
      In the lofts of the Empire
State when the painter, Ayisha,
Arrived, too late, from India.

She tried photography instead,
Accepting the invitation
      A darkroom offered, a luke-warm
Chemical bath where light might rise
As India did in her dreams.

Negatives Ammu had left her
Of the life under British rule
      Surprised her. Even wet, the prints
Gleamed, then ignited. Ayisha
Found in those black-and-white photos

Something so over bright, so dark,
A focused pain, yes, roofless walls
      And ashes, ashes just below
The silver grain, she can't go on.
But Ammu's also rising through

Her dreams, dressed up to meet the friends
Ayisha's made since Ammu's death.
    Yes, there she sits on a charpoi,
Laughing and picture pretty and
Lucid as India herself.

A SONG ON THE WALL

How might the sober
See what's written here?
       Voicelessness—maybe

Alienation. Love
Wouldn't occur
       To such interpreters.

You have to be queer,
Or passing time and
       Beer, or both, to

Read through
The crudeness of graffiti
       To the calls of men out

Searching for
Something as new as
       Our skin when we were children.

How else can I explain
The little wit
       This come-on

Contains as sufficient
To loose laughter
      From my gut? *My big cock*

wants to meet
your lips does it now—joy
      Inarticulate, proof

Some man or boy
Beyond these walls somehow
      Remains romantic.

A SONG LEARNED ON THE RED ROCKET

Was it the train's hesitation
That shook the young man I was
From his book? That let him look up, look
Out through the glass into the dark

> Tunnel where I'm sure he hummed then
> *It must be there's a red signal.*
> That was one way his winter of
> Travelling underground, keeping

His head down, started to come to
An end. Across the aisle of
That stopped subway car the eyes of
Another as young met his, eyes

> That managed, before they deftly
> Looked blank and away, to somehow
> Send, a puzzle, both the *Stop* and
> The *Proceed with Caution* signals

In the one package. The train lurched,
In reaction to its own lights,
We suppose, accelerated
Down the line and emerged. This must

Have been that exposed stretch—Yonge, you
Know, the bit below Eglinton?—
Where the banks on either side of
The ditch in the March sunlight shone

So green, our hero looked up at
The cloudless blue showing between
The skyscrapers and vowed from then
On he'd try to see past signals

And confusion—*Some enchanted*
Morning, you will across a car—
Right through to the clarity of
The ones that say *Go*, that say *Come*.

ROBERT'S SEA CHANGE

Go off on your own, they instructed you. *Turn away from each
other. By talking to no one, you will learn the essence of*

communication. One among many young men and women
In training, you were willing to follow directions (your own

Had yet to unfold) into the November chilly country
Out near Nanaimo, willing till one rock by the bay stopped you.

Did it hold itself up, hold itself out like a hand to you?
Is that how you knew you'd fit? Did it say, *Come to rest. Welcome.*

Let your wandering cease—? Did the ocean, its faces turning
Up against that shore, also reflect the face of your solitude? Is

That why all the love of water you embraced after sixteen
Summers swelled up too, a tide that carried you into the hands

Of the waves? How cold they were, even through clothes. Your
      breath leapt up
Like a fish but in a cry so vulgar, your neighbour, a young

Woman guarding both a rock and a silence of her own, broke
Out in laughter. Later she said the blur you'd been, a bobbing

Head and twitching underwater limbs, had made her fear, just that
Moment before, an octopus reaching out for her. Your curse

And less than graceful progress back onto the land transformed you
Into a mere man. Not ever a merman. Dry, almost warm

Again in your clean, pressed jeans and sweater — though the memory
Of your own thrashing through seaweed tentacles, your hard
    scrambling

Up rocks, your escape, still stung you like salt. The undertow had
Almost sucked your running shoes off, had licked a shivering so

Deep into your pores, you knew you'd begun an unfolding there.
Yes, as you cruised down, blue webs would soon have stretched
    between your toes.

She told you how a sea lion had risen up out in the bay
After you'd gone, how directionless he'd been and slow. *Oh*, you

Wondered, *Was he looking for me?* And now you're wondering too
If he might have made wet love to you, had you'd stayed there and
    changed.

HIGHWAY ABOVE VANCOUVER

Under the pearling
    Grey light drizzling down
From the ceiling of
Scud, the car—was it
    Almost in flight? Hurled
On by the tires, by

The dry cheer wiper
    Blades supplied, yes, you
—Not the driver—were
About to arrive
    At an opening
In the world. You'd left

Conversation far
    Behind and plunged on
Through mist, hopeful and
Blind, into this break
    In the weather down
Slope, onto that grey

Gleaming flat bedrock
      —The bay under rain.
Oh you looked at it
Again, at the blue firred
      Island it bore, just
Before that broken

Weather healed, closed up
      Once more by fogged-up
Glass and atmosphere,
The wings of the car,
      Yes, you looked just as
It stirred and entered

Your opening head,
      A great restlessness,
An ancient dreaming,
An image that knocked
      Your tongue into gear.
Hey, the words whirled, *there*

are gods sleeping down
      there! But the mountain's
Blank face already
Had blocked out the view
      And the driver who
Still was back where talk

Was limited to
    Only what the white
Line through runoff said
About passes through
    Mountains, thank you, didn't
Welcome the news.

IV

PLANE SONG

The hand of the mountains
Opens up below us.

The sun's crossing its palm
With a lake like a leaf.

Leaves blossoming mists
Are rare at this latitude.

It's worth a look before
The mountains close back in.

It outshines minerals
And cold—and then it's gone.

Let's carry it with us
To tell us our fortune—

Leaving the aurora
Borealis behind.

FORKED SONG

Maybe it was the snake
    Who offered up the fruit?
A choice, from what I've seen,

Never easy or nice.
    —Now I lay me down in
The middle of the road—

I bet he prayed, he hissed,
    Calming the forking of
His tongue, his instinct for

Self-preservation. How
    Long it took for God or
Us to take his offering!

The tires of some car
    Ran him over at least
Twice before his skin split

Apart and his heart slipped
    Out, solitary and
Red as meat. Not until

Its beating stopped did

It look like some berry
You might, in fact, eat. There

In the dirt his body
        Could then have been a stem
Or a vine longer than

Your arm, too far to reach.
        Is it wisdom to know
The difference between

Cooked and raw, ripe and green,
        The distance in between?
When last seen that heart had

Become a ruby still
        Attached, in our oh so
Natty world, not to

A garter but a ribbon
        You might easily sport
As a charm at your throat.

POSTCARD (FOR GEORGE) FROM MEXICO CITY

Who knew the New World was so old? Just off
      The Zocalo where that massive flag of
The United States of Mexico lifts

Up in the breeze like a tri-coloured wing,
      Beyond, behind the Cathedral, this maze
Of ruins, volcanic rock, is also

Unfolding. So the tourist, the guy whose
      Indian face (it's me, George!) shouldn't be
So out of place that a late September

Sun—this far south, this up in the mountains—
      Is able to rub it raw, this guy is
Lost, almost, and in awe. The pyramids

That once served the two gods of rain and war
      —The latter somehow both left-handed and
A hummingbird—even in this jumbled

State are so present, the evident weight
      Of an empire, of actual human
Sacrifice, it's no surprise to the tourist

How Jesus Christ fit right in. Letting Him
      Take the fall for once and all is clearly
The better deal. Back in the plaza,

Among the merchants and mariachis,
      An Aztec-costumed Indian, the high
Striped feathers of his headdress shivering,

Dances, dances, but not for a vision
      Like the priest who saw that first eagle perch
On a cactus devouring a snake

Here on the island in a lake this land
      Once was, no, he dances for the office
Workers, taking their smoke or lunch hour

Breaks from the National Palace. Of course
      He dances too for that little boy dressed
In blue sweats, perched and sighing on the curb

Till his father gets through with work. The New
      World, the new deal, allows for Aztec
To be a profession too. The tourist

(The one with the Indian face, the one
      Who shouldn't be—not here—so out of place)
Exits the ruins and enters the plate-

Glass doors of the museum and almost
        Finds himself happy in the conditioned
Air and face to faces with a wall of

Carved granite skulls, each death's head different,
        Smirks, gazes, cold stares. Yes, even in death,
That old totalitarian realm, you

Get to be an individual. Is
        There even a sort of democracy?
He laughs now at how unlikely that is.

FIRST-QUARTER BLUES

The guy'd only been
Treading water
In the rush hour and
      Went under after

The moon's first quarter
(A limestone island
In a lake of sky)
      Dropped into his head

And rings of a blue deeper
Than day's spread out
Into his blood. The sidewalk
      Tide flowed

Around him. As the lights
Changed, his body
Did too, into some
      Thing mercury strange.

The bones in his hands stretched
Down toward the mud
While overhead floated
      The crowd, stars or

Bubbles. Down he sighed
Through the layers of
Lake, his ache settling
        In with the fossils.

HARBOURFRONT EVENSONG

A bit late in the day
When the rain at last ends.
Out over the lake, clouds,
Breaking up, make a lie

Down for light. So it does,
Stretching, as well it might,
A yawn or two of hue
Above the city dark

And polished with wet. What
Point is there, remaining
Upright, trying to scrape
The sky? Who needs heaven?

Even the wind's asleep
In the west and voices
Of water insist on
Rest. Lie down? Yes. Yes. Yes.

WENDY ON THE SHORE

She unrolled her bed among rocks beside
    The Caspian Sea, just as she had all
        Those other nights in that country, unrolled

        Her bed pretending she still was feeling
    At home, pretending she felt sure the stones
Her eyes were, full of so much land, would be ·

Lighter later, the strange washed away, sand
    In the surf of sleep, rolled out that bed and
        Laid down her head in her hurry to rest.

        The familiar sounds of the Sea would
    Be her lullaby. She thought she would not
Need to try to fall asleep, thought she would

Probably be pulled under. Not a tear
    Was needed now. Her almost nightly
        Dream of her family was on the rise.

        Then the sky washed a sand of stars into
    Her eyes, a bright night vision that marked new
Constellations and more out of the dark,

A map so true, dreams were nowhere on it.
  She felt the earth take a deep breath and raise
    The rock-a-bye-ing of its body up—

    A cradle. On she turned all the way to
  Dawn, eyes open as the Sea, ears like shells
With the rhythm, her own body a baby.

A SMALL ESSAY ON THE LARGENESS OF LIGHT

for C.T.

We spend so much of our lives in darkness,
      We're comfortable there, kids under covers.
Even more so in the kind we create
      For the audience. And though lights may rise

And discover actors stepping onto
      The stage or there already in a scene,
We're not surprised by their brightness, only
      And still after all these years by their size.

Only the moon at dusk above a dark
      Horizon shows such magnification.
It's a quality that can only be part
      Of a dream, we explain, or illusion.

Look at that actor, the way he turns with
      His prop telescope toward the pinprick stars
In the backdrop sky, a gesture so huge
      Up there on the stage, it has to be true

He's the Galileo we learned about
      In school, it has to be now he's about

To divine the shape of the cosmos. Why
      Else would he be taking so much time? You

Don't suppose he just forgot his next line?
      Too cool, too comfortable, that magnified
Actor, that magnificent player is,
      For that to be fact. Oh the way he holds

The stage is a lesson in beautiful.
      It's all about star quality, he's sure,
Though like the moon, he shines by reflection.
      Looking for his light, he turns, about to

Monologue, and his Galileo gaze
      Falls through the fourth wall onto the people
Out there in the hall. His Galileo
      Eyes let him see us here as we've never

Seemed before. It's all, he's certain, about
      Vision, but for more than that, he doesn't
Quite have words, except those the play allows
      And they pull him now toward catharsis and

Conclusion. Only a spirit, let's say
      Galileo himself, proprietor
Of that lens, having been roused from his rest
      By an actor's performance—Did I not

Tell you the guy was good?—looks into
       The black auditorium (the dead do
See in the infra-red) and finds—even
       More of a surprise—the sky we are, oh

The retina shine of eyes looking back.
       Indifferent night never shook him as
Much as our eyes do, rapidly shifting
       Through a waking dream, illusion in lieu

Of disbelief. These eyes gape and even
       He finds himself reminded of the flesh.
They're closing, opening in unison,
       Taking in the action up here on stage,

The true Galileo hearing a song
       In the night. Oh how unfamiliar
Eyes have become since his death. Was ever
       He at ease with these pinprick lights, crimson

Hunger's nightmare glare piercing the backdrop
       Those bodies are? All these legions, all these
Mouths so alive in the darkness. The ghost
       Pulls the covers back up over his head.

SOME ADVICE FROM A BEAR'S BONES

Wasn't ferociousness and
Fur the ideal disguise?
  How else did we manage days
  Of hunger and nights of ice?

How else avoid the pitfall
Of family resemblance,
  Forced smiles, all broken teeth,
  The honeyed breath in rank gasps?

Yes, falling in love till death
Wouldn't ever have sufficed.
  Oh, when you pulled that blanket
  Up over your head, we laughed.

Everything you will ever
Dream or recall or forget,
  It's etched in the walls inside
  The orbits of our eyes.

It would pain you to see. Just
Imagine stars. And wrap us
  Up again in fur. Bury
  Us as if we were your own.

LAST-QUARTER SONG

How long ago did our Grandmother go
To the moon? Is it true, do you know? All

Grandmothers do when their business here is
Done? How fully there that moon is tonight

In the crystalline air. If our Grandma
Is watching over us from way up high,

Surely she can see our futures. Oh if
Only the moon's reflection, suddenly

So close on the water we've been stirring
With our paddles—oh if only it were

Our Grandma's face. Then it wouldn't matter
That the moon wanes and waxes. Its light,

New or old, would stand in for her promise
To always come back and welcome us home

From our navigation of the rivers
Of the night. We'd never lose our paddles.

THE SOLSTICE BLUES

The road's blending into
The blow and banks of snow.
      So here you are, braking
      The car in a whiteout.

The drift allows a glimpse
Or two of blue, the far
      Sky, a field, starts you
      Aching for the open.

Or you could let go, yield
To this place and end
      Your fears, find the grace here
      Of true and absolute

Zero. But no. No. Shift
Instead into low. Steer
      On through. You know that's also
      What the world will do.

HIGHWAY 99

A flag of smoke off
The factory stack
Across the sound, white

In the weatherless
Morning as the two
Of us in the car,

Midway through our drive
Up the coast, were blunt,
Half alive, almost

Blue, having passed too
Many mountains through
Our heads. Oh we stopped,

We surrendered—we stretched
Our stiffness with a walk
Down a beach

Of shadow blue
Stones and watched as
The light, coming up, coming

Down over the snow
Of the divide at
Half past ten a.m.

Reached and bleached
The stones of their shadows and
The dark of the tide.

We stood and shivered,
Hunching our backs as
The mountain top edge

Of the air, still sharp
At sea level, cut
Into our clothes. You

Scratched a match, lit
Your nth cigarette, flew
Your own unbending

Smoke. I broke into
A jog, punted a can
Down the beach past

The warnings against
Swimming and poisoned
Fish. Stones underfoot

In the light might have
Been eggs about to
Hatch. Then the sun touched

My back and I looked.
Green and rock colours
Rose on the far shore

On the headlands and
Flat black water was
Turning out ruined

But blue from the last
Of the shadow that
Was over there too.

I suddenly saw
And said I saw how
Once upon a time

People could believe
The world got reborn
Everyday. You put

Your cigarette out
With a toe, coughing
A laugh—*Once upon*

a time to get back
on the road!—And though
We nosed the car north

Through an afternoon
Long on asphalt glare,
Though we ended up

Where a tavern full
Of smoke put a stop
To the road, with shadows

Of mountains and night
So close, they might have
Soon closed us down,

I still found myself seeing
—*Another round!*—
That light from the sound.

DAUCUS CAROTA EN PASSANT

That Queen Anne who welcomed our Four
        Indian Kings to England, what
        Do we know of her—or them—now?
Wild carrot preserves only

        Her name with a lacy-headed,
Ahistorical poetry.
None of the other weeds displayed
        By the double-paned windows of

The train seems to be dropping names.
        A few descendants of those Chiefs
        Know and usually are pleased to
Tell the story, how the silver

        Communion service Anne gave them
—Some portions of which still rest in
Her Majesty's Royal Chapel
        Of the Mohawks, used mostly for

Irregular Sunday worship—
        Was still intact at the end of
        The Revolutionary War,
The pieces having been buried

To frustrate looting. Only then
Were they divided like the Six
Nations themselves between those who
     Followed Brant into Canada

And those who remained behind in
     The Haudenosaunee homeland.
     In the country this other side
Of Lake Ontario, riding

     Among goldenrod and tasselled
Grasses, crushes of rushes and
Bloodless blue chicory florets,
     The Four Kings all but forgotten

—As is Brant's Anglican passion—
     What Anne's vegetal namesake seems
     Able to offer commoners
Like us, though not quite deluxe, not

     The usual tarnished silver,
Is enough. This late in August
Her lace laid in place, doilies the
     Décor for a rail right of way,

Now will also do, as you see,
　　　　For an altar rail, will be the
　　　　Comme il faut cloths even those up
Front in VIA One First Class can't

　　　　Help but experience as meet
And right. A nod overnight from
The frost curled enough of Queen Anne's
　　　　Flowers up into chalices

Which even she'd have wished to use
　　　　If she'd once come slumming this way.
　　　　Let's lift up these burnished cups and
Salute with a toast all that is

　　　　Divided, every thing that's lost.
The late summer air slakes our thirst,
Stops our aches. In our windy wake,
　　　　The drying grass falls on its knees.

IN THE MONTH OF MAY

How generous
Wild roses
Are, tendering

A scent to who—
Ever's running
By. And the gift

They offer
Your eye! From the shade,
This blue blush, see—

Through as rain,
Washes you to
A standstill, empty

Of aching breath,
Destination,
Everything—

Acknowledgements

Most of these poems, or earlier versions of them, appeared previously thanks to the editors or directors of these periodicals, books, sites or performances:

absinthe
The Antigonish Review
ARC Canada's National Poetry Magazine
The Art of Living, the 2006 Prague-Manitoulin Island-Toronto Project
The Book of George (The BoG Collective, Department of Film,
  Theatre and Creative Writing, University of British Columbia)
Border Crossings
Canadian Literature
Canadian Theatre Review
The Church-Wellesley Review
CV2 Contemporary Verse
Edges of Time (Seraphim Press)
ELQ/Exile The Literary Quarterly
event magazine
The Fiddlehead
Gatherings
Lifeworlds – Artscapes, Contemporary Iroquois Art (Galerie 37
  Museum der Weltkulturen)
Literary Review of Canada
Maisonneuve Magazine
Maisonneuve.org

Next Exit
Prairie Fire
Poetry Canada Review
Quarry Magazine
Quint (University College of the North)
The Returning the Gift Anthology (University of Arizona Press)
Siolence (Quarry Press)
Poetry Toronto
Whetstone
Without Reservation, Indigenous Erotica (Kegedonce Press)
Yellow Medicine Review